THE
GIANT
PLANETS

THE GIANT PLANETS

ALAN E. NOURSE

FRANKLIN WATTS
NEW YORK / LONDON / TORONTO / SYDNEY / 1982
A FIRST BOOK / REVISED EDITION

Cover photograph of Saturn and
some of its moons courtesy of NASA

Interior photographs courtesy of
Bettmann Archive, Inc.: p. 10;
NASA: pp. 12, 16, 24, 30,
38, 42, 45, 46, and 51,

Diagrams by Vantage Art, Inc.

Library of Congress Cataloging in Publication Data

Nourse, Alan Edward.
The giant planets.

(A First book)
Bibliography: p.
Includes index.
Summary: Discusses the discovery and features of
the large outer planets of our solar system.
I. Planets—Juvenile literature.   [1. Planets]
I. Title.
QB639.N68   1982   523.4   81-21812
ISBN 0-531-00816-9   AACR2

CONTENTS

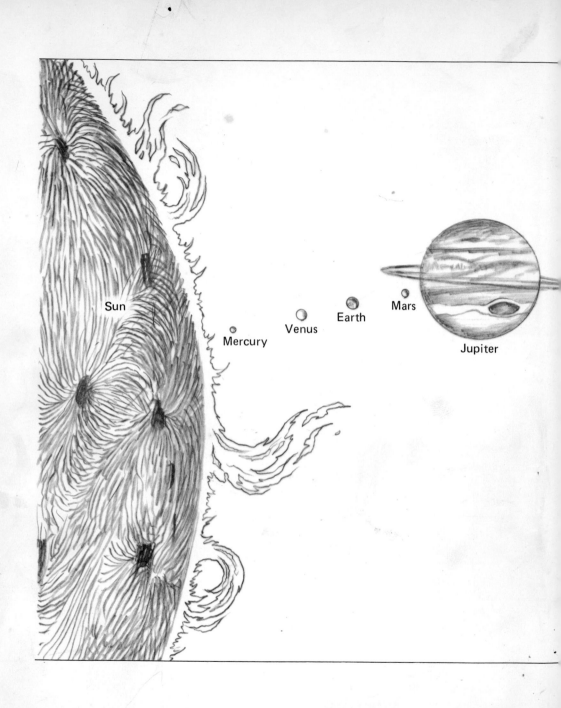

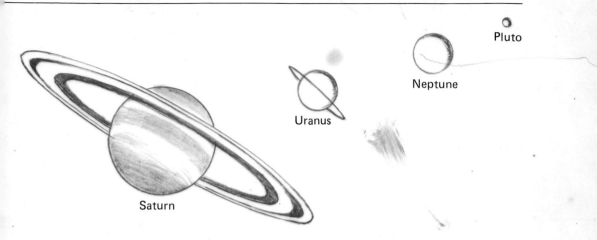

Pluto

Neptune

Uranus

Saturn

**Positions of the Planets
in Relation to the Sun**

CHAPTER ONE

THE REALM OF THE GIANTS

One evening many years ago, a scientist in northern Italy was studying the heavens with a new instrument he had just constructed. Although he may not have known it then, he was about to make one of the most exciting discoveries of his career.

The year was 1610. The scientist was Galileo Galilei, already known for his brilliant studies on the force of gravity. The instrument he was using that night was an "optik tube," a device similar to the first crude telescopes invented in Holland just two years earlier. But Galileo's telescope was much more powerful than the Dutch instruments. It could magnify heavenly objects as much as 32 times and had already shown Galileo many things he could never have seen without it. For example, he had observed huge craters on the moon and had discovered that the planet Venus often showed a strange crescent shape in the sky, like a tiny crescent moon.

But when Galileo peered through his telescope at the planet Jupiter, he discovered something even more remarkable. To the unaided eye, this "wandering star," so long familiar to ancient stargazers, looked like nothing more than

Galileo Galilei, 1564–1642

a brilliant point of light in the sky. But through the telescope, Galileo could see a definite disk, like a small gold coin in the sky. What was more, Jupiter was not traveling alone in the heavens. The telescope revealed four tiny pinpoints of light lying close beside the planet, so small they could not be seen at all without magnification. But there could be no mistaking what they were. These four tiny lights were, in fact, four separate moons circling the planet Jupiter, in much the same way our own moon circles the earth.

Galileo was not by any means the first observer to pay special attention to this bright golden object in the sky. Astronomers had known for centuries that this was no ordinary star. Over many thousands of years, ancient stargazers had learned to recognize certain familiar groups of stars in the sky, known to us today as *constellations.* The ancient astronomers knew that the stars in these constellations might all rise or set together in the course of a night, or be present in one season and sink below the horizon in the next. However, they always remained in the same position in the sky in relation to neighboring stars.

A few special objects, though, behaved differently. These so-called "wandering stars" did not occupy fixed positions in the heavens like the other stars. Instead, they seemed to travel at night in straight lines, circles, or even zigzags against the backdrop of the constellations. Because of their strange patterns of motion, ancient stargazers gave special names to these objects and paid special attention to their movements.

Five of these "wandering stars" were known in ancient times. One of them seemed to move especially rapidly from night to night, and so it was named Mercury, after the swift messenger of the gods. Another that became silvery bright at certain times was named Venus, for the goddess of love and beauty, while ruddy Mars was named for the god of war. The two remaining "wanderers" moved much more slowly in the sky, taking months to change their positions. These were named for Jupiter, the ruler of the gods, and for Saturn, Jupi-

ter's father and a god associated with agriculture. For many
centuries, ancient astronomers plotted the motion of these five
celestial objects, even though they did not understand why
they were different from the other stars or why they moved
about in the sky when the other stars appeared to be fixed.

THE SUN AND ITS PLANETS

Today we know that these five are not really stars at all but
planets, a word that comes from the ancient Greek word meaning "wanderer." Our own bright sun is a star. Other stars look
different to us because they are so very far away. Some are
larger than our sun, some are smaller. Some shine with an
intense blue light, while others have a more reddish glow than
our own yellow sun. Like our own sun, these stars are all
moving (around the galaxy, that is), but they seem always to
remain in the same position in the nighttime sky because of
their great distances from us.

The planets are far closer to us than even the nearest star,
for they are members of our sun's own family of planets, which
we call the *solar system*. The ancient astronomers knew of only
five of these planets in addition to the earth—the five that
could be seen with the unaided eye. It was only after powerful
telescopes were invented that three more planets—Uranus,
Neptune, and Pluto—were discovered and named.

We now know that the planets of our solar system are different from stars in some very important ways. Unlike stars,
which shine with their own light, the planets give off no light of

Jupiter (top right)
and the four moons
first seen by Galileo,
now often referred to
as the "Galilean moons."

their own. What we do see is the light from the sun that the planets reflect back to us. In addition, each one of the nine planets in our solar system is traveling in its own special path, or *orbit,* around the sun, held in place by the powerful force of the sun's gravity, very much as if it were a ball speeding around the sun at the end of a long string.

Finally, most stars are so very far away that they never appear to us as anything but pinpoints of light, even when observed through powerful telescopes. But the planets, which are much closer to us, can be seen in the telescope as coin-shaped disks. Some of them can even be seen to have surface markings similar to those we can see on the face of the moon on clear nights.

STUDYING THE PLANETS

Over the centuries, as a result of careful study, observation, and measurement, scientists have learned a great deal about the planets of the solar system. Telescopes were a giant step forward. They revealed to astronomers the truth about the structure of our solar system.

Today's astronomers have many kinds of instruments available to aid them in their studies of the solar system. Modern telescopes are equipped with cameras to make permanent photographic records for storage and careful analysis. An instrument known as a spectroscope enables scientists to detect the presence of gas in the atmosphere of a planet and to determine in which direction the planet is rotating. Radar signals are used to explore the surface of distant planets, and modern radio telescopes can tell us if radio waves are being emitted by a planet. Still more sophisticated instruments, such as magnetometers and charged-particle detectors, which are used to study the regions of space around the planets, plus special TV cameras for taking close-up photographs, can be mounted on exploratory spacecraft destined for close encounters with the planets.

As a result of all we have learned from such instruments, we now know that all of the planets have certain things in common. For example, we know that each planet's orbit around the sun is in the shape of a slightly elongated oval known as an *ellipse.* What is more, each planet is also constantly turning on its own *axis*—an imaginary line drawn through the planet from its north pole to its south pole—as it orbits the sun. The earth, for example, rotates on its own axis once every 24 hours. Mercury, the closest planet to the sun, turns on its axis only once in approximately 58½ days, while mighty Jupiter whirls around on its axis in slightly less than 10 hours.

We also know that each planet's orbit lies very nearly on the same flat level, or *plane* (a mathematical word for a perfectly flat surface), as the plane of the earth's orbit. This is known to scientists as the *plane of the ecliptic.* Jupiter's orbit, for instance, lies almost exactly on the same plane as the earth's. Mercury's orbit is tilted slightly away from the plane of the ecliptic, a matter of 7°. Only distant Pluto's orbit is tipped more than Mercury's. Astronomers would say that Pluto's orbit is *inclined.* It is tilted about 17° from the ecliptic, the greatest amount of tilting of any of the planets. Thus, although a model of our solar system seen from above would seem very large in diameter, it would appear very thin and saucer-like when observed edge-on, because each of the planetary orbits lies on approximately the same plane as all of the others.

THE TWO KINDS OF PLANETS

As astronomers gathered more and more information about the solar system over the years, they soon came to realize that the planets could be divided into two quite different groups, or families. The first group, including Mercury, Venus, the earth, and Mars, is made up of comparatively small, heavy planets composed of large quantities of rock, metal, and other dense materials. Because these four planets are all so similar to the

Graceful Saturn, as seen by Voyager 1 on October 18, 1980. The colors have been enhanced by a computer to reveal surface features.

earth in structure, astronomers call them the *terrestrial,* or "earthlike," planets, from the Latin word *terra,* meaning "earth." They are also known as the *inner planets.*

In sharp contrast to these small, dense planets, there are four other planets in the solar system that are so remarkably different from the earth in size and structure that it is hard to believe they could be planets of the same sun. In fact, these planets—Jupiter, Saturn, Uranus, and Neptune—form a family of giants far more similar to each other than to any of the terrestrial planets. They move in orbits much farther from the sun than the four inner planets, and they are truly huge by comparison. For example, Jupiter, the largest of the giants, has a diameter more than 11 times the diameter of the earth, while the diameter of Uranus, the smallest of the giants, is still over 3 times the earth's diameter. What is more, all of these giant planets are incredibly lightweight in spite of their huge size. The reason for this is that they are made up, in large part, of extremely light substances such as hydrogen, helium, methane, ammonia, and water-ice.

Because these *outer planets* in the solar system are so huge and are composed so largely of gas, astronomers have come to call them the *gas giants.* Only one planet, Pluto, is farther from the sun than the most distant of these gas-giant planets. So far, no one is entirely sure what Pluto is like, but most astronomers believe that it resembles the terrestrial planets more than the gas giants.

EXPLORING THE GAS GIANTS

For many centuries, the only way that scientists could learn about any of the planets of the solar system was by means of telescopes or other instruments located here on earth. With the beginning of the space age in the 1950s, however, rocket engines were developed that were powerful enough to lift instruments and later even human crews into space to study neighboring parts of the solar system at close hand. Until the early 1970s, however, the distant giant planets remained almost as mysterious as they were in Galileo's time.

Then, on the evening of March 2, 1972, one of the most exciting real-life space adventures of all time began to unfold, when a tiny robot spacecraft named *Pioneer 10* was launched from Cape Canaveral, Florida, to begin an actual voyage out to mighty Jupiter and beyond. Followed by its sister ship, *Pioneer 11,* and later by two larger *Voyager* spacecraft, *Pioneer 10* spearheaded humankind's first on-the-spot, close-up exploration of the realm of the giants. In the years that have passed since they were launched, those four adventuring ships have already sent back many answers to our lingering questions about these giant planets—and raised many fascinating new questions in the process. In the following chapters we will see how the *Pioneer* and *Voyager* ships were launched on their great adventure—still going on today—and then look more closely at each of the giant planets in turn, together with their families of satellites, to see what we have learned and what we still don't know about them.

CHAPTER TWO

PIONEERS
AND
VOYAGERS

It's a long, long way from the earth to Jupiter.

Whenever we start to talk about the vast dimensions of our solar system, we soon find ourselves in trouble. The distances from one planet to another are so very great, they are almost impossible to imagine. This is not such a problem with the comparatively nearby planets, such as Mars and Venus. But when we start considering the realm of the giant planets in the vast outer reaches of the solar system, the enormous distances involved become almost meaningless. Modern astronomers can tell us that Jupiter's orbit is an average of 483 million miles (773 million km) from the sun—some 390 million miles (624 million km) farther from the sun than the earth is. But these numbers can mean very little to us.

To grasp the staggering reaches of space between us and the nearest gas giant, we first need some kind of yardstick for comparison. Consider, for instance, the *time* it might take us to travel to Jupiter on a purely imaginary space voyage. Suppose for a moment that you were a passenger aboard a fully equipped spaceship heading straight out from the sun in a journey that would take the ship through the orbits of each of the planets of the solar system in turn. Suppose that ship is traveling in a straight line at a steady speed of 5,000 miles (8,000 km) per hour—several times faster than the swiftest supersonic transport plane of today, but still a speed we can imagine. This way, our imaginary ship would cross the orbit of each successive planet in the shortest time the ship's speed would allow. How long, then, would it take our ship to reach the orbit of Jupiter?

The answer may seem surprising. First, of course, we would cross the orbit of Mercury, the innermost planet, some nine months after the journey began. Continuing on our way, we would approach the orbit of Venus approximately ten months later and would encounter the earth's orbit some seven months after that, nearly twenty-six months—two years and two months—from the beginning of the journey.

At that point, however, because the planets' orbits are progressively farther apart, the travel time from one orbit to the next would be progressively longer. Zooming past the earth at an unslackening speed of 5,000 miles (8,000 km) per hour, our ship would take another full year to reach the orbit of Mars— three years and two months since the beginning of our journey. Then, leaving Mars behind, we would move out across a vast gulf of space, with the monotony relieved only by the sighting of an occasional stray asteroid. Presently, the ship would enter the so-called *asteroid belt,* an area of space containing a multitude of rock and metal fragments, some as tiny as grains of sand, others as large as mountains or even larger. Yet even at this point, far out beyond the orbit of Mars, after five and a half solid years of traveling, our voyage to mighty Jupiter would only be half done. From this point on, our ship must plunge forward for another five and a half years before, at long last, the sphere of Jupiter is reached and the first stage of our journey is near an end.

Certainly Jupiter at this close a range would be a breathtaking sight to behold. But in terms of time—already eleven years of traveling behind us—our imaginary voyage to the orbits of the gas giants would hardly have begun! Racing on past the king of the giant planets, our spacecraft would have to cross a truly stupendous void of empty space, traveling for another full nine years before finally approaching the orbit of Saturn, second-largest of the planets and by far the most beautiful of the gas giants—a total of twenty years since beginning our solar system tour. On beyond Saturn, the ship would take twenty-one *more* years to reach the orbit of Uranus, and an additional twenty-three years to approach Neptune, outermost of the known gas-giant planets. A baby born on our ship the day it started on its journey from the sun would be *sixty-four years old* on the day we reached Neptune.

THE PATH OF THE PIONEERS

Of course, the journey we have just described is purely imaginary, intended only to demonstrate the vast distances that separate our own, inner neighborhood of terrestrial planets from the mighty gas giants beyond. Real spaceships don't travel in straight lines. After *Pioneer 10* and *11* were launched in 1972 and 1973, each traveled out from the earth's orbit in a long, graceful curve toward their distant flyby encounters with Jupiter. Because their powerful rocket boosters were capable of accelerating them to a speed of more than 31,000 miles (49,600 km) per hour before their fuel was exhausted, each made the trip to Jupiter in slightly less than two years. Each launching had to be timed precisely so that Jupiter—constantly moving in its own orbit all the time the *Pioneer* ships were approaching —would be in exactly the right place to meet the tiny spaceships when they arrived.

The *Pioneers* were probe ships in every sense of the word. They were going where no human-built spacecraft had ever gone before. Each carried about 55 pounds (25 kg) worth of scientific instruments, including sending and receiving radio equipment, television cameras, and devices for measuring temperatures, magnetic fields, and radiation in the ship's vicinity. But basically, the *Pioneers* were intended to answer two major and critical questions. First, could spaceships actually navigate the hazards of the asteroid belt and arrive at Jupiter without being smashed to pieces? And, if they did reach Jupiter, could their delicate instruments survive bombardment by the charged particles and the intense magnetic field known to surround the mighty giant?

Astronomers had known for years that a vast belt of asteroids—tiny planets, if you will—traveled in orbit around the sun between Mars and Jupiter. The larger asteroids, hundreds of miles in diameter, had been sighted in telescopes and even named. But many scientists feared that there might be billions upon billions of tiny asteroids, perhaps no larger than rocks or grains of sand, and that any ship passing through the area might simply be punched full of holes and thus totally destroyed. There was no way to tell except to send a ship there to find out.

Jupiter's magnetic field, discovered in 1955 by astronomers working in earthbound laboratories, was even more of a potential hazard. Like the earth itself, Jupiter was known to be a huge magnet in space. But the size and intensity of the magnetic field surrounding Jupiter was believed to be far more powerful than the earth's. Such a magnetic field might do funny things to delicate electronic instruments—perhaps wreak such havoc that nothing at all could be learned from close flybys of the giant planets. Again, the only way to find out was to send a ship there to see.

The *Pioneers* passed both tests with flying colors. Both ships zoomed through the asteroid belt without even a single asteroid collision. On December 3, 1973, as *Pioneer 10* moved in to its closest approach to Jupiter, just 80,000 miles (128,000 km) above the cloudtops of the giant planet, it was jarred repeatedly by shock waves caused by Jupiter's magnetic field, and its scientific instruments were knocked temporarily out of kilter. But they quickly recovered and sent accurate data about the area speeding home to earth. Because of this success, scientists decided to alter *Pioneer 11's* course slightly by firing its small guidance rockets. This would make the second ship pass even closer to Jupiter. On December 2, 1974, just a year after *Pioneer 10's* flyby, *Pioneer 11* whizzed past Jupiter a mere 21,000 miles (33,600 km) above the cloudtops—and again, all instrument systems continued to function.

The mission of the *Pioneers* was over—and 100 percent successful. Crude TV images of Jupiter and its major satellites had been transmitted back to earth, and many scientific studies had been performed. Aided by Jupiter's powerful gravitational tug, *Pioneer 10* was then greatly speeded up and shifted off course, sending the little ship on a new path that would take it completely out of the solar system, perhaps to wander among the stars forever. A golden plaque carrying drawings of human beings and symbols of human knowledge was added to the little ship before launching on the chance that someday, in the unimaginable future, intelligent creatures in other parts of the universe might find it and be able to tell where it came from and who sent it. *Pioneer 11's* course was more sharply twisted by Jupiter's gravity, so that once its flyby mission with Juplter was accomplished, it was hurled outward in the solar system for a rendezvous with Saturn, a meeting that took place in September 1979. As of late 1981, both ships were continuing on their new courses, all their instruments still functioning beautifully far beyond their expected lifetimes.

VOYAGERS *AHOY!*

The *Pioneers* proved one thing beyond doubt, that the giant planets could indeed be explored in very close and dazzling detail. But even as the *Pioneer* ships were still on their way to Jupiter, space scientists were working frantically to prepare two larger, more sophisticated spacecraft, *Voyagers 1* and *2*, for launching toward the giant planets in the late 1970s.

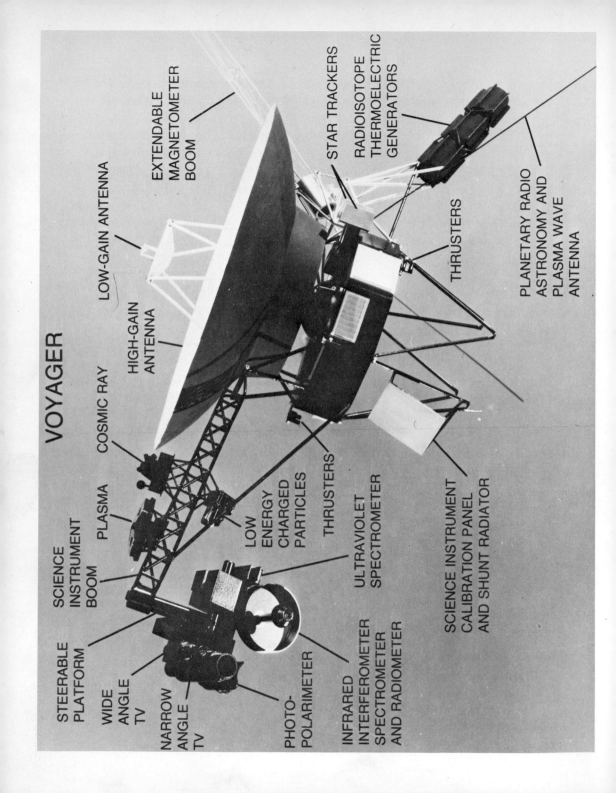

VOYAGER

STEERABLE
PLATFORM

SCIENCE
INSTRUMENT
BOOM

COSMIC RAY

PLASMA

WIDE
ANGLE
TV

NARROW
ANGLE
TV

PHOTO-
POLARIMETER

INFRARED
INTERFEROMETER
SPECTROMETER
AND RADIOMETER

ULTRAVIOLET
SPECTROMETER

LOW
ENERGY
CHARGED
PARTICLES

THRUSTERS

SCIENCE INSTRUMENT
CALIBRATION PANEL
AND SHUNT RADIATOR

HIGH-GAIN
ANTENNA

LOW-GAIN ANTENNA

EXTENDABLE
MAGNETOMETER
BOOM

STAR TRACKERS

RADIOISOTOPE
THERMOELECTRIC
GENERATORS

THRUSTERS

PLANETARY RADIO
ASTRONOMY AND
PLASMA WAVE
ANTENNA

There was a very special reason for the urgency of these new exploratory missions. As we have seen, scientists knew that the powerful gravitational field of Jupiter could seize a close-approaching spaceship like a giant slingshot and literally hurl it on outward into the solar system with greatly increased speed toward the planets beyond. Further, it was known that a most unusual planetary situation would exist during the late 1970s and early 1980s—an opportunity too good to miss. During these few years, all of the giant planets would be lined up in their orbits around the sun in such a way that a single spaceship, launched at the right time, could conceivably make a "Grand Tour" of all four on a single trip. Thus, a single extended voyage could send back detailed pictures and information about each one of the giant planets in turn. Such an opportunity would not arise again for another 175 years!

Voyager 1, about the size of a compact car, was much heavier than the tiny *Pioneer 10* and carried a large number of scientific instruments. It was launched on the first stage of its possible "Grand Tour" on September 5, 1977, and it flew by Jupiter on March 5, 1979. *Voyager 2* was actually launched two weeks earlier than *Voyager 1,* on August 20, 1977. But its slightly different route of travel brought it to its Jupiter flyby a little later, on July 9, 1979. Both ships then moved on toward Saturn, with *Voyager 1* arriving at the heavily ringed planet in mid-November 1980 and *Voyager 2* rendezvousing with Saturn in late August 1981.

Astronomers and space scientists had some very definite ideas of what would be found when the sophisticated *Voyager* spacecraft made their respective encounters with Jupiter and Saturn. Yet what actually was discovered by those ships proved many scientific ideas to be totally wrong. In each case, old theories had to be discarded, and new and exciting facts were discovered. In the next chapters we will look at some of the exciting discoveries of the *Voyager* missions.

CHAPTER THREE

JUPITER, KING OF THE GIANTS

During late February and early March of 1979, a large number of astronomers and other space scientists from all over the world gathered in growing excitement at the Jet Propulsion Laboratory at the California Institute of Technology in Pasadena, California. The reason for the gathering—the imminent flyby of *Voyager 1* past Jupiter, providing the closest-ever look at that giant planet and its family of satellites. Many of the scientists gathered thought they already knew quite a lot about the largest planet of the solar system. In the next few days, they found out that much of what they "knew" was wrong, while things they had never even dreamed of turned out to be true.

Of course, scientists did know certain things about Jupiter and its satellites before *Pioneer* and *Voyager* data began coming in. For instance, they knew that the diameter of Jupiter, measured at the equator, was some 88,600 miles (141,800 km) —over 11 times the earth's 7,900-mile (12,600-km) diameter. This means that Jupiter is by far the largest planet in the sun's family. Indeed, this one planet is so very huge that it contains more matter than all the other planets of the solar system put together!

In spite of its great distance from the earth (the two planets never come closer to each other than 370 million miles, or 592 million km), Jupiter sometimes appears as a brilliant object in the nighttime sky. In fact, it reflects so much sunlight from its huge disk that only Venus and our own moon appear brighter to us. As we might expect, Jupiter moves much more slowly in its orbit around the sun than the inner planets. Although it travels in orbit at a velocity, or speed, of 8 miles (12.8 km) every second, its orbit is so huge that the planet takes 11.86 earth years to complete a single turn around the sun. This means that the earth, moving much faster in a smaller orbit, is constantly overtaking Jupiter and then passing it by. As a result, conditions are good for observing Jupiter from the earth for a good part of each earth year.

Astronomers have also known for some time that, despite its long and ponderous journey around the sun, Jupiter's "day" —the time it takes to make one complete turn on its own axis —is surprisingly short. Jupiter makes one complete rotation every 9 hours and 55 minutes. This swift rotation has a curious effect on the shape of the planet and its atmosphere. The equatorial regions, for example, bulge outward, and the polar areas are flattened, so that the planet looks for all the world like a huge, slightly squashed beach ball.

THE SURFACE MARKINGS

Scientists observing and photographing Jupiter's disk through earthbound telescopes had long been fascinated by the bands of light and dark clouds that could be seen on its surface. Some of these bands had been seen so consistently that they seemed like old friends. Astronomers had even given them special names. Jupiter's equator, for example, is marked by a narrow band of dark clouds known as the equatorial band. Above and below this are zones of lighter clouds known as the equatorial zones. Other belts of clouds that had remained visible year after year include the north and south tropical zones, which form wide colored bands on the planet's surface, and darkened areas known as the north and south polar regions. It was believed that these cloud belts represented only the outermost surface layers of an incredibly thick, dense cloud layer pressing down upon Jupiter's surface. No one really knew, though, what those clouds were made of.

In addition to the bands of clouds encircling the planet, the disk of Jupiter presented another puzzle that had mystified astronomers for centuries—a huge, oval-shaped spot in the cloud layers first observed by the French astronomer Jean D. Cassini in the year 1665. In contrast to the yellowish color of the rest of the planet, this spot at first appeared a pinkish-red in color. Then, over the years, its color seemed to deepen until, by 1878, it had become a dark, brick-red. Since then, this so-called *Great Red Spot* has remained almost constantly visible, although its color seems to fade at certain times and become more intense at other times. Certainly, the Spot is huge. It was estimated, in fact, to be some 26,000 miles (41,600 km) long and 8,000 miles (12,800 km) wide—big enough to drop the whole planet earth into without touching the edges! But what *was* it? It remained for the *Voyagers* to tell us.

Finally, before data from the *Pioneer* and *Voyager* spacecraft began flowing back to earth, astronomers were aware that mighty Jupiter had a family of *satellites,* or moons, circling it, just as the planets of our solar system circle the sun. In addition to the four major moons of Jupiter known since Galileo's time, nine other smaller satellites had been discovered with earthbound telescopes. Most astronomers assumed that the smaller moons were little more than very large rocks, and that the four major satellites would all be dead—pockmarked spheres similar in nature to the earth's own moon, perhaps encrusted with thick layers of water, ammonia, or methane ice, but not exceptionally interesting nor different from one another. It was in this area more than any other that the *Voyagers* proved our scientific guesswork most dramatically wrong.

CLOSE-UP OF JUPITER
The earlier flybys of the *Pioneers* brought the first hints that much of what scientists had believed of Jupiter and its satellites might be proved wrong. But the true picture didn't emerge in all its wonder and beauty until the *Voyagers* paid their visits to the king of the giants.

As *Voyager 1* began its close approach to Jupiter in the early months of 1979, the first, most striking thing revealed by its TV cameras was the wide variety of colors in the bands of clouds circling the giant planet. The fuzzy light and dark bands previously observed from the earth and by *Pioneer 10* now resolved themselves into bands of brown, orange, and dark red as well as yellow, gray, and white. At still closer range, these colored bands were seen to be masses of roiling clouds high up in Jupiter's atmosphere, driven from west to east or east to west by savage winds endlessly circling the planet at speeds of up to 340 miles (540 km) per hour. Only occasionally could one see through breaks in these clouds to observe darker clouds in the lower parts of the atmosphere. The cloud activity was most intense in the equatorial and tropical zones; only the polar regions seemed relatively quiet. Pictures taken from the night side of Jupiter revealed enormous lightning storms high up in the atmosphere, as well as auroras much like our own northern lights, caused by charged particles from the sun interacting with Jupiter's huge and intense magnetic field.

The Great Red Spot was discovered to be a storm, a huge, perpetual whirlwind, much like our own hurricanes here on earth but on a far grander scale. Sometimes, smaller storms would be caught up in the great red whirlwind and passed around its edge. Similar, smaller whirlwinds—mostly white in color—were pinpointed by the *Voyager* cameras and followed as they raced around the great planet.

Of course, all of these surface features, violent as they seem, are merely a thin coating of gases on the top of the cloud blanket covering Jupiter. What *Voyager* was recording with its TV cameras was only "weather"—but what weather! These clouds were made up mainly of hydrogen gas at temperatures of around 200° below zero, F (-130°C). In addition to hydrogen, the outer atmosphere contained significant amounts of helium, as well as smaller amounts of ammonia ice crystals, methane gas, and water-ice crystals. The many colors of the surface layers are believed to be due to small amounts of impurities mixed in at different levels.

But what lies beneath these clouds? Deep below the cloud surface, *Voyager* instruments detected rising temperatures and vastly increasing pressures due to the weight of the atmosphere pressing down. Indeed, the center of this giant planet is so hot that Jupiter is now known to be throwing off *twice* as much energy in the form of heat as it receives from the sun.

Scientists now believe that beneath the outermost layer of clouds, which are a few hundred miles thick, Jupiter has a very dense layer of hydrogen and helium in liquid or gaseous form. There is no solid surface as we would normally think of it, just a supercompressed soup of liquid hydrogen thousands of miles thick. Still deeper, pressures become so extreme that the hydrogen is probably compressed into a dense, solid, metallic layer even thicker than the layer above. And finally, at the very

Jupiter's Great Red Spot
(upper right) *seen close up.*
The black and white inset shows
Jupiter with its Great Red Spot
(lower middle) *turned toward us.*
Note in the color photograph
all the roiling clouds in Jupiter's
stormy upper atmosphere.

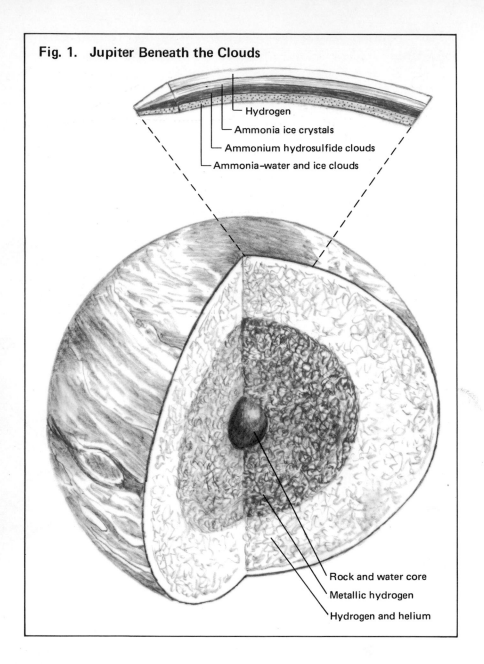

Fig. 1. Jupiter Beneath the Clouds

— Hydrogen
— Ammonia ice crystals
— Ammonium hydrosulfide clouds
— Ammonia–water and ice clouds

Rock and water core
Metallic hydrogen
Hydrogen and helium

center, making up less than one tenth of the interior, there may be a relatively tiny core of solid rock and water.

The *Voyagers* confirmed other things that were known or suspected about Jupiter. There is indeed a powerful magnetic field surrounding the planet. Electrons and other charged particles moving through this magnetic field create huge belts of radiation like the so-called Van Allen belts surrounding the earth. These particles also account, in part, for powerful blasts of radio waves that Jupiter sends out from time to time. Other bursts of radio static are triggered by the movement of one of Jupiter's moons, Io, around the planet. In fact, a burst of radio "noise" occurs with every revolution.

Another *Voyager* discovery, however, was completely unexpected—the fact that Jupiter is surrounded by a thin, disk-shaped ring made up of a swarm of dustlike particles. This ring is so delicate that it could be seen by *Voyager* only when the mighty planet was directly in front of the sun. Some of the most amazing *Voyager* pictures of Jupiter showed that ring and revealed its presence for the first time.

IS THERE LIFE ON JUPITER?

At one time astronomers believed that the regions beneath Jupiter's cloud layers would be far too cold to support any kind of life. Now, the suspicion is that temperatures deep beneath the clouds might be far too *high* to support life as we know it, to say nothing of the crushing atmospheric pressures there.

With elements under its seething surface
that make it more like the sun than the earth,
Jupiter is probably nearly 9/10 hydrogen.
Its small rock core may be covered by metallic hydrogen.
Above that, hydrogen and helium mix with traces of other
substances to create the dense clouds that cover Jupiter.

—33

Yet strangely enough, it is not unreasonable to think that some form of life, however unearthly, might exist on Jupiter. We know, for instance, that there are sea creatures on earth living in the depths of the ocean at pressures far greater than any land creature could tolerate. And, we know that the hydrogen, water, ammonia (a nitrogen compound), and methane (a carbon compound) making up the cloud banks of Jupiter are all building blocks for life as we know it. The rich colors of Jupiter's clouds as revealed by *Voyager* photographs could well be due to complex organic molecules (molecules that make up living things), possibly built up under pressure during the raging electric storms that occur in Jupiter's upper atmosphere.

Unfortunately, the *Voyager* probes could cast little real light on this question. We will have to wait until devices are dropped down through the obscuring clouds to take samples and measurements before we can do more than guess whether or not life of any sort could exist there.

EXPLORING JUPITER'S MOONS
Thus, bit by bit, our exploring spacecraft built up a picture of a strange planet indeed, totally alien and mysterious in comparison to anything we know here on earth. If it were possible for human explorers to float down through Jupiter's cloud layers in spite of the increasing pressure and other dangers, they would find a strange world constantly torn apart by violent hurricane-force winds. Beneath the cloud banks, they would encounter a vast ocean of liquid hydrogen, methane, and ammonia, perhaps with huge "mountain ranges" of solidified hydrogen emerging like storm-torn islands. It would be a perilous place, a dimly lit half-world so utterly hostile to humans that even the frigid moons of the planet would look inviting by comparison.

But what about those frigid moons of Jupiter? Here, at least, space scientists thought that the *Voyagers* might find something vaguely familiar—moons that might be similar in many ways to the earth's own moon. They could not have been more wrong.

Thirteen moons of Jupiter were known at the time the *Voyagers* were launched. The four largest—Io, Europa, Ganymede, and Callisto—were the ones Galileo first discovered by peering through his primitive telescope hundreds of years ago. A very tiny fifth satellite, discovered in 1892 by Edward E. Barnard and known as Amalthea, travels in orbit only about 68,000 miles (109,000 km) above the top of Jupiter's cloud banks. Later, eight more satellites were discovered, all so small (ranging from 6 to 75 miles or 9.6 to 120 km in diameter) that they could not have been detected by the unaided eye even if you were on a ship in close orbit around Jupiter!

The *Voyagers* added two new members to Jupiter's family of known satellites. *Voyager 2* pictures of Jupiter's rings were later found to reveal a midget fourteenth satellite some 25 miles (40 km) in diameter traveling in orbit *inside* the orbit of Amalthea, about 34,000 miles (54,400 km) above Jupiter's cloudtops. This tiny chunk of rock, now known as Adrastea, whizzes around the giant planet once every 7 hours and 8 minutes. Other *Voyager* pictures identified a fifteenth satellite, still officially known as 1979-J2, in orbit about halfway between Amalthea and Io, revolving around Jupiter every 16 hours.

No one was especially surprised at the discovery of these two new moonlets of Jupiter, but the four planet-sized Galilean moons brought plenty of surprises. Far from the frigid, many-cratered bodies scientists had expected, *Voyager* data revealed that each of these four major moons differed markedly from the others—and indeed, from all other bodies in the solar system as well.

Take Io, for example, the innermost of the four and about the size of the earth's moon. In close-up pictures, Io looked just like a huge pizza, its surface wildly mottled in reds, oranges, pale yellows, browns, and blacks. Early during the *Voyager 1* encounter, an enormous bright plume was discovered rising above the satellite's surface—an active volcano in the process of erupting in an explosion 5 times more violent than any ever seen on earth! Before *Voyager 1* moved on past Jupiter, seven more major erupting volcanoes were identified. When *Voyager 2* arrived four months later, only one of the eight volcanoes sighted earlier had fallen dormant, and two new ones were spotted. Io was by far the most volcanically active planetlike body known anywhere in the solar system, and the *only* body other than the earth known to have any such activity at all.

In between the volcanoes, Io's surface was unmarked by any of the impact craters of the sort that scar the surface of the earth's moon. The yellow and red coloring and smooth surface, scientists believe, is due to repeated showers of frozen sulfur dioxide and sulfur dust, resulting from the constant volcanic eruptions. These cover up any impact craters that might form.

The next major moon, Europa, presented a totally different picture to the *Voyager* cameras. In contrast to the wild reds, yellows, and blacks of Io's surface, the surface of Europa, slightly smaller than Io, appeared placidly white and unmarked. No active volcanoes. Only a few worn-down impact craters. A moon slightly smaller than the earth's own and completely covered with ice. But close views reveal that the ice is cracked and crumbled in long fracture lines that crisscross the entire surface. Scientists now speculate that Europa's icy crust may be as much as 60 miles (96 km) thick, completely surrounding a rocky interior.

The third major moon, Ganymede, is the largest of them all—3,270 miles (5,232 km) in diameter. It is one and a half times as large as the earth's moon, larger even than the planet Mercury and now known to be some 90 miles (144 km) larger in diameter than Saturn's giant moon Titan. This makes Ganymede the largest moon in the solar system, and even after the *Voyagers'* close encounters, it remains one of the most mysterious. Part of Ganymede's surface is pockmarked with impact

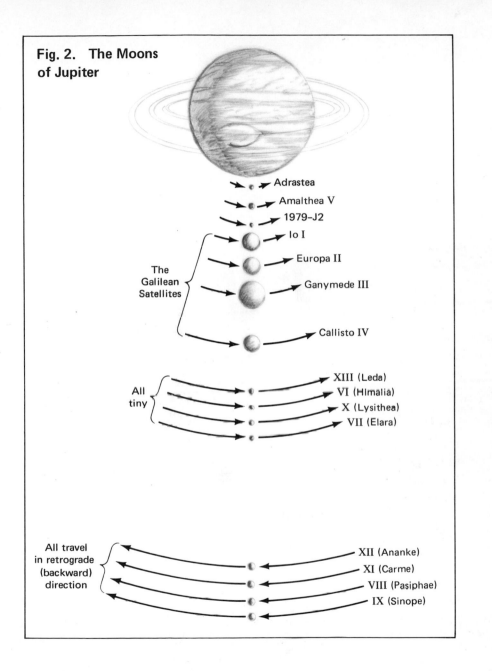

Fig. 2. The Moons of Jupiter

Adrastea

Amalthea V

1979–J2

Io I

Europa II

The Galilean Satellites

Ganymede III

Callisto IV

All tiny

XIII (Leda)

VI (Himalia)

X (Lysithea)

VII (Elara)

All travel in retrograde (backward) direction

XII (Ananke)

XI (Carme)

VIII (Pasiphae)

IX (Sinope)

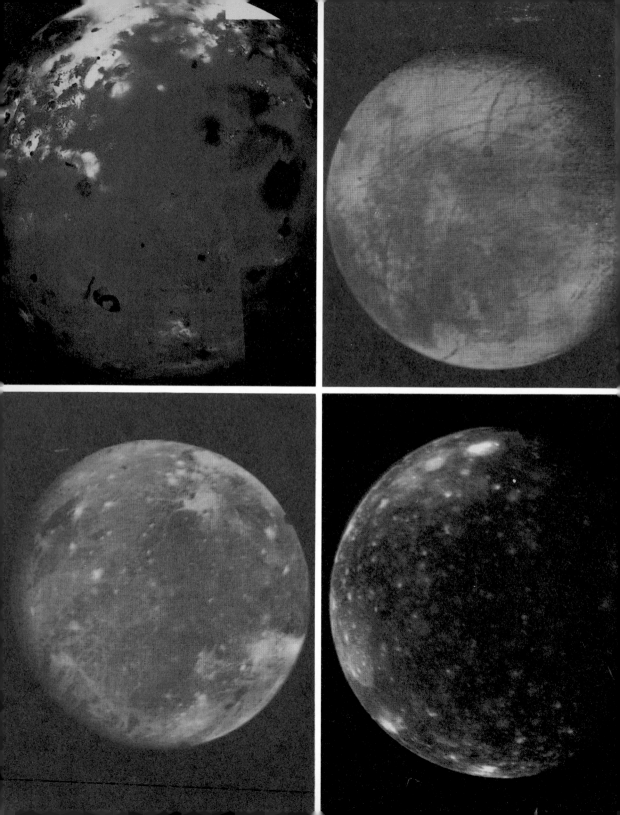

craters caused by meteorites; some of these craters appear very old, some more recent. But other parts of the surface appear smooth, with distinct light and dark areas. One huge dark spot covers fully one third of one side of the satellite. And in other areas, *Voyager* pictures revealed vast networks of grooves and ridges that branch, weave, and intersect with each other. The best guess today is that Ganymede contains a large inner core of rock or metal, completely blanketed in a coating of ice hundreds of miles thick.

Callisto, the outermost of the Galilean satellites, is slightly smaller than Ganymede but still larger than the earth's moon. It is the only one of Jupiter's moons that really resembles our own satellite. Its surface is literally peppered with meteorite impact craters—perhaps more so than any other body in the solar system—with no sign of internal activity wiping away any of the impact evidence. Even Callisto's impact craters have impact craters, believed by some scientists to be as much as 4.6 billion years old. Indeed, although large parts of Callisto were not photographed in detail by the *Voyagers,* this cold, ancient, ice-covered moon may turn out to be a virtual museum of solar system history and development, its pockmarked surface essentially unchanged since the earliest days of planet formation.

THE STAR THAT NEVER WAS

Certainly, from what we have learned of Jupiter's moons from the *Voyager* explorations, these giant satellites all seem rather

The Galilean moons.
Upper left: *Io*
Upper right: *Europa*
Lower left: *Ganymede*
Lower right: *Callisto.*

forbidding and hostile places. Manned landings on any of them would be most unlikely in the near future. But how did the great Jupiter system, with its gas-covered giant planet and its own "solar system" of moons come to be formed in the first place?

Astronomers today believe that when the sun and its planets first began to form from clouds of interstellar gas, not one but several stars tried to form. Only one, our sun, gathered in enough dust and became big enough and hot enough to finally ignite the continuing chain of thermonuclear reactions necessary to turn it into a true star. A second huge gathering of matter in the same general region of space—Jupiter—never quite succeeded.

At its birth, Jupiter may have been hot enough to glow for a while and throw off some light of its own, but it could never have shone like a star. It simply never had enough material to become hot or dense enough to ignite self-sustaining nuclear reactions. If it had, our sun would have become a double star, and the solar system as we know it today might never have developed.

As the *Voyagers* swept past Jupiter and its moons, each in turn, they sent back more knowledge of this gas giant in a few weeks than scientists had collected in 400 years. At the same time, Jupiter's gravity acted like a giant slingshot on each of the *Voyagers,* turning them in their courses and hurling them at increased speeds farther out into the solar system. The next rendezvous, almost a year and a half later and a billion miles (1,000 million km) farther out, would be with the second of the gas giants—the spectacularly beautiful and intriguing planet named Saturn and its many moons.

CHAPTER FOUR

SATURN, JEWEL OF THE SOLAR SYSTEM

For its first encounter with Saturn, the second largest and by far the most breathtakingly beautiful of the gas giants, the *Voyagers* had to cross a truly stupendous void of empty space. Jupiter lies an incredible 483 million miles (773 million km) from the sun, but the orbit of Saturn is almost *twice* as far—a staggering 886 million miles (1,417 million km) away. Thus, after *Voyager 1* swung past Jupiter in early March 1979, it did not reach Saturn until twenty months later, in mid-November 1980. *Voyager 2* flew by Saturn in late August 1981.

If anyone had been aboard *Voyager 1* or *2* on its long trip out from Jupiter, he or she would have seen some remarkable things. Day by day, the sun would have seemed to dwindle in size and brightness, unmistakable evidence of the vast distance the little ships had traveled. At the same time, the great golden disk of Saturn would have grown larger and larger in appearance. Compared to Jupiter or the other giant planets, Saturn would have seemed particularly spectacular, for the great globe of this planet is permanently surrounded by a series of brilliant, light-reflecting rings. These rings extend for hundreds of thousands of miles and are almost blindingly

—41

*Saturn as seen by Voyager 2.
In this photograph we can see the
marked tilt of the gaseous giant.*

bright when seen from above or below. Yet when viewed edge-on, they are so thin that they can hardly be seen at all.

When Galileo first viewed Saturn through his telescope in the year 1610, he was perplexed. Unlike Jupiter, the planet's disk seemed oddly shaped and mysteriously different from one observation to the next. The puzzle was solved in 1655 when a Dutch astronomer named Christian Huygens, armed with a more powerful telescope than Galileo's, saw that the strange appearance of Saturn was due to a system of rings girdling the planet. When seen at an angle, these rings looked like an oval-shaped golden halo around the equator. Early astronomers saw only two separate rings in the system, with what they thought was a vast area of empty space between them. That space was called *Cassini's Division,* after Jean D. Cassini, the astronomer who first described it. Two hundred years later, a third ring was observed within the outer two, called the Dusky Ring or the Crepe Ring because of its faintness and the difficulty with which it was seen. Some later observers thought they could see a fourth, outermost ring, even more faint than the Crepe Ring, but other astronomers doubted its existence. If they had only known!

SECOND OF THE GIANTS
Before the *Voyager* flybys of Saturn, what scientists knew about the planet was very similar to what they knew—or thought they knew—about Jupiter, except that Saturn was almost twice as far from the sun and thus had to be much colder.

Saturn is indeed another giant planet, with a diameter of approximately 75,000 miles (120,000 km) as measured at the equator. This is somewhat smaller than Jupiter but is still large enough to dwarf the earth, with its 7,900-mile (12,640-km) diameter.

Being of such gigantic size, Saturn contains far more matter than all of the terrestrial planets put together, but the material that makes up this giant planet is so very light that astronomers believe Saturn would actually float if it could be dropped into an ocean of water big enough to hold it. Like Jupiter, it is made up mostly of very light elements and compounds such as hydrogen, helium, ammonia, water-ice, and methane, with only a comparatively tiny core of heavier, more solid materials such as iron or rock.

Because Saturn is so much farther from the sun than Jupiter is, its orbit around the sun is much bigger, and the planet travels in its orbit much more slowly than the inner gas giant. In fact, it takes Saturn almost 29½ earth years to make a single trip around the sun. With such slow and stately motion, Saturn does not travel through much of its orbit in the course of one earth year, so that the earth in its own orbit is constantly "catching up" with Saturn and then passing it by. This means that Saturn, like Jupiter, is visible to stargazers here on earth for a long period each year.

As one might expect, Saturn receives less heat from the sun than Jupiter does, yet oddly enough it gives off comparatively more heat from its interior. Rather than having cooled off ages ago, as scientists had once assumed, Saturn is still radiating more heat into space than it receives from the sun. Unlike Jupiter, the yellow giant is tilted rather markedly on its axis, so that it has regular "seasons" in the same way the earth does. On the other hand, Saturn, like Jupiter, is surrounded by a powerful magnetic field and spins on its own axis almost as fast as Jupiter does, so that a "day" on Saturn lasts only a little more than 10 hours.

Saturn also has "weather" much like Jupiter's—terrible "weather" indeed, as *Voyager 1* discovered on its close approach in November 1980. Scientists were not surprised to learn that Saturn was surrounded by vast belts of storm-driven clouds of hydrogen, helium, water-ice, and ammonia—beautiful bands of pale yellow and tan clouds in the equatorial and temperate regions of the planet, with billowing white clouds

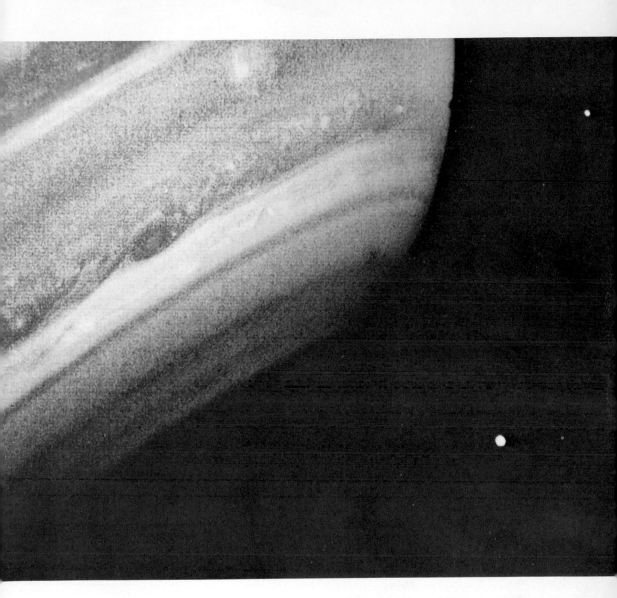

*In this closeup of Saturn, two
of the moons can easily be seen—
Dione (upper right) and Enceladus.*

obscuring the polar regions. There was even a huge pink oval-shaped whirlpool storm just below the equator, much like Jupiter's Great Red Spot, only smaller and paler. Other, somewhat smaller whirlpool storms were also spotted by *Voyager 1* cameras. Nor was anyone surprised when other studies suggested that Saturn beneath its thick clouds was much the same in structure as Jupiter—layers of liquid hydrogen, helium, and liquid ammonia hundreds of miles deep, with an even deeper layer of solid metallic hydrogen, probably surrounding a tiny core of rock and metal.

Most of these similarities to Jupiter were expected long before *Voyager 1* reached the vicinity of Saturn. What was not expected was the close-up appearance and behavior of Saturn's mysterious rings.

THE STRUCTURE OF THE RINGS

As we have seen, before the *Voyager* approach, Saturn was thought to have three, perhaps even four, broad rings girdling its equator, each separated by wide areas of empty space. What *Voyager 1* revealed was a far more spectacular system of rings—hundreds of rings, possibly even *thousands* of them, spread out as much as 169,000 miles (270,000 km) from one outer edge to the other, with the innermost rings fairly skimming the cloud cover of the planet itself. Cassini's Division and other "empty" spaces between groups of rings were found to be filled with ring particles. Most of the rings were perfectly

Four Voyager 2 *photographs
of Saturn's magnificent rings.*
Upper left: *A Ring;*
Upper right: *C Ring;*
Lower left: *F Ring;*
Lower right: *some rings seen to
the south of Saturn's cloudtops.*

—47

circular, but others were slightly oval or elliptical, their courses taking them right through the circular ones. Two rings in the outermost ring region, known collectively as the F Ring, even appeared to be braided or twisted around each other in an intricate pattern!

What are the rings made of? Astronomers still can only guess. Many reflect a great deal of light, others reflect very little. The best bet is that the rings are made up of untold trillions of icy particles ranging in size from microscopic bits on up to giant snowballs 3 feet (1 m) in diameter, with each particle moving in its own individual orbit around Saturn. The majority of these particles and fragments may be nothing more than balls of water-ice or frozen ammonia. Others may be ice-covered rocks, even huge boulders—a terrible hazard to any spacecraft that might be hit by one. One thing is certain, however. Wide as this complex ring system may be, it has hardly any *thickness* at all. *Voyager* scientists guess that the rings may well be no more than about 10 miles (16 km) thick, some possibly no thicker than 30 or 40 inches (about 80 cm)!

THE MOONS OF SATURN

Like Jupiter, Saturn has a family of natural satellites, or moons. Before the *Voyager 1* encounter, astronomers using earth-bound telescopes had identified and named ten major satellites.

If we look at these moons in order of ascending size, we begin with tiny Janus, no more than 200 miles (320 km) in diameter and only 50,000 miles (80,000 km) from the planet's cloud layers and just slightly beyond the outermost ring. This

Voyager 1, *in 1981,*
discovered five additional
minor moons of Saturn.

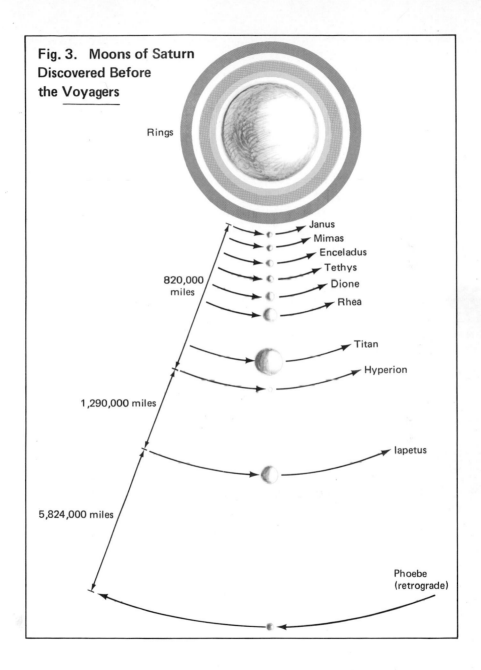

Fig. 3. Moons of Saturn
Discovered Before
the Voyagers

Rings

Janus
Mimas
Enceladus
Tethys
Dione
Rhea

820,000 miles

Titan

Hyperion

1,290,000 miles

Iapetus

5,824,000 miles

Phoebe
(retrograde)

tiny moonlet is so close to the rings of Saturn that it was completely missed until 1966, when French astronomer Audouin Dollfus discovered it while the rings were turned edge-on to earth. After Janus comes Mimas, 115,000 miles (184,000 km) from Saturn's surface and 320 miles (512 km) in diameter. Third is Enceladus, 148,000 miles (236,800 km) out and 460 miles (736 km) in diameter. Tethys, with its orbit 183,000 miles (292,800 km) from Saturn and measuring about 650 miles (1,040 km) in diameter—about one third the size of the earth's moon —is fourth, and fifth is Dione, 234,000 miles (374,400 km) out. Dione is about as far from Saturn as the earth's moon is from the earth and 700 miles (1,120 km) in diameter. Sixth is Rhea, 327,000 miles (523,200 km) out and 950 miles (1,520 km) in diameter, and seventh is Titan, one of the largest of all the moons in the solar system, 3,180 miles (5,088 km) in diameter and 759,000 miles (1,214,400 km) from the surface of Saturn.

Up to this point, the known moons of Saturn seemed to follow an orderly sequence, each larger and farther out than the next. But beyond Titan this orderly pattern is broken. The next satellite out, far from being larger than Titan, is a midget. Called Hyperion, this moon is a mere 300 miles (480 km) in diameter and 918,700 miles (1.4 million km) from Saturn. Then there is a vast expanse of empty space, over 1¼ million miles (2 million km), before we reach Iapetus, moving in its orbit over 2 million miles (3.2 million km) from Saturn but only some 900 miles (1,140 km) in diameter. Finally, at the outermost limits,

Some of Saturn's more interesting moons. Upper left: Mimas; Middle: Enceladus; Upper right: Hyperion; Lower left: Iapetus; Lower right: Tethys.

—50

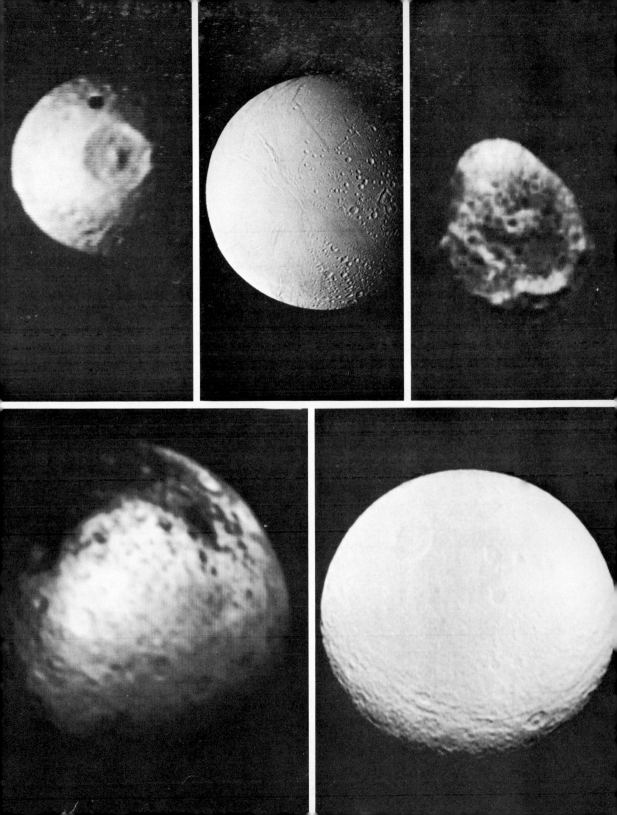

some 6 million miles (9.6 million km) from Saturn, is Phoebe, a tiny moonlet barely 200 miles (320 km) in diameter and moving in its orbit in the opposite direction from the rest!

Voyager 1 discovered at least seven additional moons of Saturn. Not surprisingly, they were all relatively tiny chunks of ice-covered rock or perhaps even solid ice, some so irregular in shape that they looked like broken teeth. What was surprising was that most of these new little moons were found to be very close indeed to Saturn's ring structure, in some cases actually *within* the ring structure. Two were discovered in virtually the same orbit just outside the rings and very close to each other, with the one behind catching up to the one ahead like a hound chasing a rabbit. Astronomers suspect that these two moons might actually collide sometime in the early 1980s. Two other moons lie just inside and just outside the "braided" F Ring, perhaps forcing the particles of those rings to remain in their curious orbits. A fifth of these tiny moonlets is farther out, apparently sharing the same orbit with Dione.

What about the larger inner moons? The *Voyagers* returned remarkably clear photographs of Mimas, Enceladus, Tethys, Dione, and Rhea. All except Enceladus appeared heavily pockmarked with impact craters, especially Rhea. Some showed radiating patterns of debris from places where especially large meteorites hit, perhaps billions of years ago. Mimas has one impact crater so huge that it covers more than a quarter of the diameter of the entire moon. Only Enceladus has a relatively smooth surface, possibly because some source of internal heat has been acting to erode its surface features. All of these satellites are probably composed mainly of water-ice and ammonia-ice, possibly cloaking tiny cores of rock or metal.

Of all the moons of Saturn, Titan has always roused the most interest. It is the second largest satellite in the solar system, half again larger than the earth's moon. Even before the *Voyagers,* scientists suspected that Titan might be the only known satellite in the solar system to possess an atmosphere, probably composed mainly of ammonia and methane gas. *Voyager 1* photos were disappointing; all they really showed was that Titan's surface was indeed completely hidden by a dense layer of atmospheric haze. The only remarkable detail to be seen was a dark "hood," or cloud, overlying the northern pole of the satellite. The tantalizing question of what Titan's surface may be like, and whether or not any form of life might have developed there, must await the time when instrument probes can be dropped down through the cloudy atmosphere. As for the outer satellites, no explanation was found for the fact that one side of Iapetus is pitch black while the other side is snow-white. In addition, *Voyager 2* revealed tiny, mishapen Hyperion to also be a puzzle, since its axis is tilted away from Saturn, in apparent defiance of the laws of orbital motion.

OUTWARD BOUND AGAIN

As *Voyager 2* was on the dark side of Saturn, the first mishap of the mission occurred, when one of the probe's movable instrument platforms jammed, causing the cameras to point in the direction of empty space. Since the incident occurred while the ship was crossing the ring plane, scientists think that a tiny ring particle might have been responsible for the jamming. Fortunately, most of the scheduled pictures had already been taken, and the platform was eventually made to work again.

Scientists will be studying the data the *Voyagers* sent home to earth for many years. But what about the outer gas giants, Uranus and Neptune?

Voyager 1's work is done. Already it has swung out of the orbital plane of the solar system in a direction that will take it toward the stars. But because of its success, *Voyager 2* was sent on to Uranus. By current calculations, it should reach the planet by late January 1986, and if all is still going well, it will rendezvous with Neptune in 1989. In the next chapter we will have a brief preview of what *Voyager 2* might find when it reaches these dim outer giants.

CHAPTER FIVE

URANUS, NEPTUNE, AND BEYOND

Voyager 2, having completed its flyby of Saturn, once again embarked on its long and lonely journey to make contact with the outer gas giants. Uranus lies even farther out from Saturn's orbit than Saturn lies from the sun, and Neptune's orbit is more than equal that distance beyond Uranus. Indeed, the orbit of Uranus is 1 billion 778 million miles (2,845 million km) from the center of the solar system, and distant Neptune is no less than 2 billion 793 million miles (4,469 million km) from the sun. Considering these great distances, it is rather surprising that we know as much as we do about these lonesome outer giant planets—especially when we realize that astronomers didn't even know they existed until 200 years ago.

THE DISCOVERY OF URANUS AND NEPTUNE

Uranus and Neptune were completely unknown to ancient stargazers. Saturn was the most distant of the "wandering stars" that they were able to distinguish. Uranus can be seen with the unaided eye as a faint pinpoint of light in the sky—*if* the observer knows exactly where to look for it and when. But this dim and faraway object is usually lost in a multitude of stars and moves so very slowly in its vast orbit that it is virtually indistinguishable without the aid of powerful telescopes. Neptune, more distant still, cannot be seen at all with the unaided eye.

How, then, were these distant planets discovered? Actually, Uranus was found quite by accident. During the spring of the year 1781 in England, a then-unknown amateur astronomer named William Herschel was studying the stars in the vicinity of the constellation Gemini, the Twins, with a home-made telescope. To his surprise, he found an object in the sky that seemed quite different from the stars near it. Most stars, no matter how close or how distant, never appear in a telescope as anything but pinpoints of light. This object had a definite disk, as if it were a planet. Since no planet was expected to be in this region of the skies, Herschel assumed that he had merely stumbled upon a new comet. After many years of study, he was able to calculate the "comet's" orbit and found it was almost circular and lay far beyond the orbit of Saturn. Only then did Herschel realize that his "comet" was actually a very distant planet of the solar system. Other astronomers confirmed his conclusion, and the newly discovered planet was named Uranus, after the father of Saturn. Uranus was the mythological god of the skies.

It was not long, however, before Herschel and other observers noticed that there was something strange about the motion of this planet in its orbit. Instead of moving placidly and slowly along, as expected, Uranus seemed at times to slow down much more than it should have, then speed up faster than it should have—exactly as if there were something tugging at it! The only thing that scientists could imagine that might be "perturbing" Uranus in its orbit was the gravitational field of yet another undiscovered planet, in this case a giant planet that lay still farther from the sun than Uranus. Two astronomers, J. C. Adams of England and Urbain J. J. Le Verrier of France, worked out mathematically where such an unknown planet ought to be in order for it to have such an effect on the motion of Uranus. Their work was a triumph for mathematical astronomy, for when scientists with powerful telescopes searched the predicted patch of sky, they soon discovered the blue-green disk of the mysterious planet beyond Uranus and named it for Neptune, the god of the seas.

STUDYING THE DIM GIANTS

Today, astronomers know a number of interesting facts about these distant, shadowy gas giants. Giant planets they are, with families of satellites much the same as Jupiter and Saturn. But they are so far from the sun that relatively little can be seen of them. In a telescope, Uranus shows as a faintly greenish disk, with markings that look like shadowy gray belts around the planet's equator. These markings are far too indistinct, however, to be useful in checking the rotation of the planet on its axis. (Surface features are often used to determine rotation periods.) Uranus is some 29,300 miles (46,900 km) in diameter, considerably smaller than Saturn, and it appears slightly flattened at the poles and bulging out at the equator, like Jupiter. Astronomers are convinced from their observations that the material making up Uranus is considerably more dense than that of Jupiter or Saturn, and that its surface is much colder, never rising above a temperature of about 310° below zero, F (−192°C). Its greenish-blue tint is believed to be the result of great quantities of methane gas in its atmosphere, and its structure is probably much the same as that of Jupiter and Saturn, including huge amounts of methane, frozen ammonia, and solidified hydrogen. With its great distance from the sun, Uranus creeps sluggishly around its vast orbit, taking 84 earth years to make one circuit around the sun. But similar to the other gas giants, it turns on its own axis in an interval of some 10 hours and 45 minutes.

In two respects, however, Uranus is known to be a fascinating oddball among the solar system planets. For one thing, in the late 1970s the planet was observed to have a system of rings similar to the rings of Saturn, though perhaps on not quite as grand a scale. So far, nine rings have been identified.

In another respect, Uranus is truly unique among the planets of the solar system. As we have seen, many of the planets tilt slightly on their axes. The earth, for example, has a tilt of 23½°, which accounts for the seasonal climate changes we experience throughout the year. Jupiter is hardly tilted at all, a mere 3°, while Saturn tilts almost 27°. By comparison, Uranus is tilted clear over on its side, with an inclination of 98°! This means that the planet appears to be rolling along in the direction of its orbit like a bowling ball going down a bowling alley. And since the rings and moons of Uranus are arranged neatly in the same plane as the planet's equator, they revolve in their orbits around Uranus like the spokes on a ferris wheel!

What about these moons? We know very little about them except that they are there, at least five of them, beginning with tiny Miranda, which has a diameter of some 150 miles (240 km) and lies very close to the planet. Moving outward, we find Ariel, Umbriel, Titania, and Oberon, with diameters measuring 600, 400, 1,000, and 900 miles (960, 640, 1,600, and 1440 km) respectively. None of these moons has any atmosphere that has been detected, and all of them are no doubt frigid, inhospitable places, with their rocky surfaces buried under deep layers of permanently frozen ammonia and methane. Uranus would surely seem a remote and lonely outpost to any exploratory team that might one day venture that far—a desolate planet, utterly uninviting and so far from the center of the solar system that the sun would appear no brighter than any other bright star in the sky. But perhaps *Voyager 2* will bring us a whole new outlook on this planet.

THE FARTHEST GIANT

If Uranus is lonely and desolate, how much more so Neptune must be! We really know only the most basic facts about this

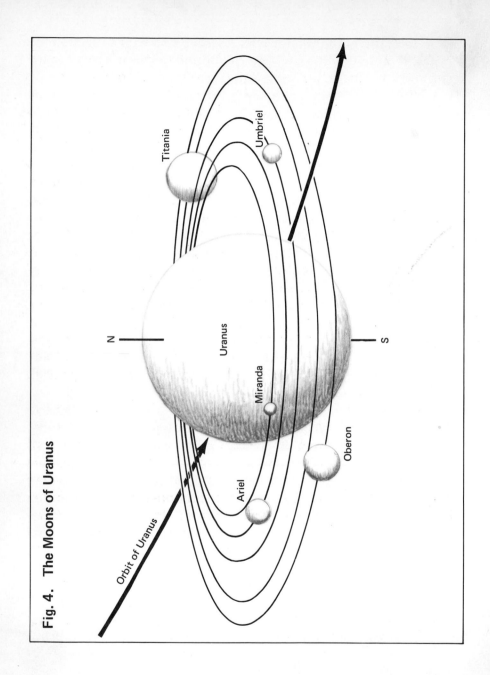

Fig. 4. The Moons of Uranus

very distant gas giant. In a telescope, Neptune's disk has a bluish-green hue, but any details on its surface are exceedingly hard to distinguish. For many years, astronomers thought that Neptune was slightly smaller than Uranus, with a diameter of some 27,000 miles (43,200 km). Recent studies completed by G. E. Taylor of Greenwich Observatory in England, however, indicate that Neptune is actually slightly larger than Uranus, and that its true equatorial diameter is some 31,000 miles (49,600 km)—almost exactly 4 times the diameter of the earth. Like the other three gas giants, Neptune has a thick gaseous atmosphere, but it is probably so very cold at the surface—360° below zero, F (−220°C)—that any ammonia present in its atmosphere has undoubtedly been frozen out. Thus, the cloud banks surrounding the planet are probably composed of methane and hydrogen, perhaps with great clouds of frozen ammonia "snow" carried in hurricane-force winds around the planet. The interior of the planet is likely to prove much the same as Uranus, with a core either of rock or solid hydrogen. This is probably surrounded by a layer of ice many miles thick, with a slushy surface of frozen ammonia giving way to the poisonous gases in the atmosphere.

Neptune also has a family of satellites, but only two have been observed so far—the huge moon Triton, over 3,000 miles (4,800 km) in diameter and only 229,000 miles (366,400 km) from the surface of Neptune; and tiny Nereid, barely 200 miles (320 km) in diameter and traveling around Neptune in a rakish orbit that seems more like the orbit of a comet than of a moon. Nereid's orbit is tilted very steeply from Neptune's equatorial plane and moves in as close as 1 million miles (1.6 million km) to Neptune and as far out as 6 million miles (9.6 million km).

THE MYSTERY OF PLUTO

These, then, are the four known giant planets—Jupiter, Saturn, Uranus, and Neptune. But where does distant Pluto fit into the scheme of the solar system? No one knows for sure.

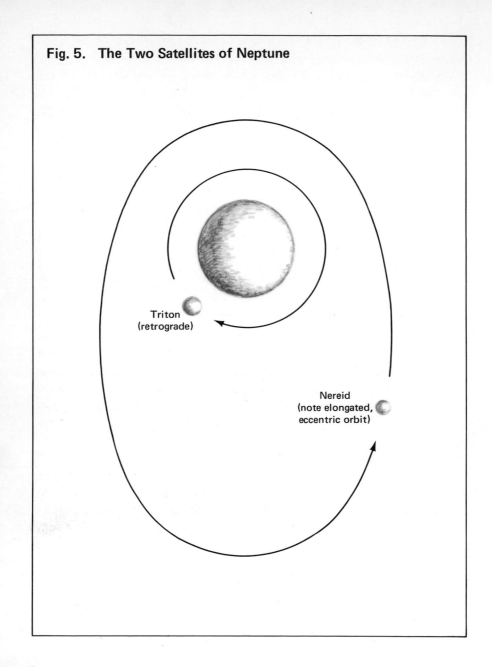

Fig. 5. The Two Satellites of Neptune

Triton
(retrograde)

Nereid
(note elongated,
eccentric orbit)

Like Neptune, Pluto's existence was deduced before the planet was discovered. After Neptune had been located and its orbit traced, many astronomers felt that this distant, shadowy gas giant had to be the last of the planets of the solar system. But, as observations of the travels of Uranus and Neptune in their orbits continued, it soon was discovered that both of these planets were again wandering slightly off their predicted course. This fact suggested that there might be yet another planet located in an orbit far out beyond Neptune. This mysterious "Planet X" was thought to be a particularly huge gas giant in order to have such a strong gravitational effect on Neptune and Uranus, which were at least 2 billion miles (2,000 million km) away from it.

In 1905, the American astronomer Percival Lowell tackled the problem of predicting the orbit of this planet beyond Neptune, but Lowell failed to locate the planet itself before his death in 1916. Other astronomers also failed in their search. It was not until January 1930 that another American astronomer, Clyde Tombaugh, finally identified the mysterious Planet X on a series of photographic plates. This planet, so dim it could hardly be seen by even the strongest telescopes, betrayed its presence on telescopic film. From the film it was clear that the planet had moved slightly against a fixed background of stars.

Tombaugh's new planet was quickly named Pluto, after the mythological god of the underworld. The name seemed particularly appropriate, for Pluto was indeed a resident of the dark regions of deep space, its orbit some 3 billion 660 million miles (5,460 million km) from the sun, almost a full billion miles farther out than distant Neptune. But as the study of this mysterious planet progressed, facts about it began to emerge that made the planet appear even more mysterious.

For one thing, its orbit was very strange for a planet of the sun. It was tilted more than 17° from the plane of the earth's ecliptic, and its orbit was far more eccentric—that is, more oval-shaped and off-center—than any other planet's orbit. In fact, it soon became clear that Pluto's orbit actually cuts across Neptune's at certain times, so that part of the time in its path around the sun, it is closer to the sun than Neptune is, while at other times it travels as far out as 2 billion miles (3,200 million km) beyond Neptune. It moves so slowly in its orbit, and its orbit is so huge, that Pluto takes over 248 earth years to make a single trip around the sun.

Certain other things about Pluto proved even more peculiar than its tilted, eccentric orbit. Although the planet matched up splendidly with Percival Lowell's prediction of its location, it did not appear to be a giant planet at all. In fact, early studies indicated that this dark planet was a solid ball of matter that was only 6,500 miles (10,400 km) in diameter—less than the diameter of the earth. Later studies indicated that this early estimate was far too large, and that Pluto was probably only about 3,600 miles (5,800 km) in diameter, much smaller than the earth and even smaller than Mars. But how, then, could such a midget of a planet so disturb the travels of Neptune and Uranus in their orbits?

Even today, no one has the answer to that question. Some argue that Pluto, though small, has a structure totally different from any of the other planets. They say that it is made of materials so exceedingly dense and heavy that it can have a powerful gravitational effect in spite of its tiny size. But the only material known that might be heavy enough to qualify would be the densely packed matter thought to exist at the hearts of dying, burnt-out stars. Others speculate that Pluto may have a very smooth surface, and that what we are seeing is only a tiny amount of its reflected light, like the small point of light reflected from a much larger billiard ball. This means that Pluto's real diameter, not yet measured, may be much larger than we think. Finally, there are those who believe that Pluto is just what it seems to be—a small, light planet with no gravitational influence at all. In fact, some astronomers suspect that the discovery of Pluto was really a pure coincidence, and that

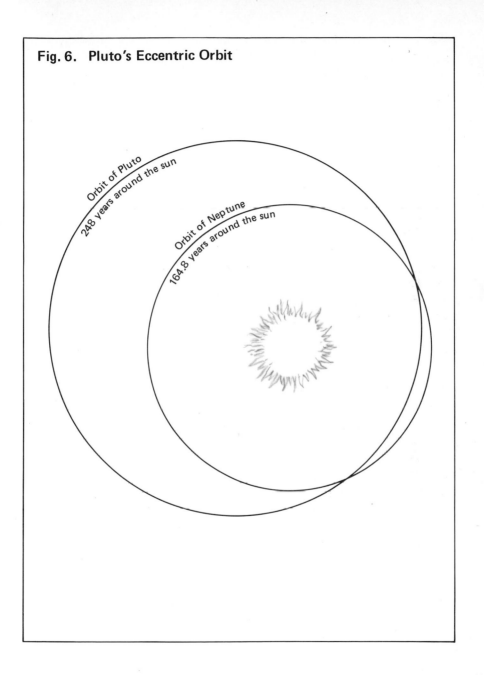

Fig. 6. Pluto's Eccentric Orbit

Orbit of Pluto
248 years around the sun

Orbit of Neptune
164.8 years around the sun

there is yet another planet still farther out in our solar system, a giant planet of staggering dimensions capable of influencing the travels of Uranus and Neptune in their orbits.

AFTER VOYAGER

No flyby of Pluto or beyond is on the drawing boards at the present time, but humankind's exploration of the solar system will certainly not end as *Voyager 2* completes its mission with a Uranus or Neptune flyby. Many grand schemes have been considered—and discarded—by our space scientists. The exploration going on today is very exciting, and the world is reaping a rich harvest of knowledge from it, but the program has been costly. Future missions will be carefully selected to gain the most knowledge at the least cost. One such project, known as Galileo, is already in the planning stages, although the ship *Galileo* will probably not be launched before 1986. As now conceived, *Galileo* would be a semipermanent unmanned observatory ship, to be placed in orbit around Jupiter. From there, acting as sort of a space platform, it could send remote-controlled sensing devices down beneath Jupiter's cloud layers, and, possibly, an instrument package down into Jupiter's sea of liquid hydrogen.

What about manned exploratory journeys out to Jupiter and beyond? Most space scientists today believe that it is still premature to think about sending humans out to the giant planets. Nearly fifty unmanned reconnaissance missions were sent out to earth's moon before the first manned landings were attempted. Surely no such journey to Jupiter will be undertaken until we have learned much more about the planet and its moons from space probes. Yet these same scientists also believe that in the long run if we *can* explore these planets firsthand, we *will,* sooner or later. It seems doubtful on the basis of what we know now that any attempt will be made to land on Jupiter's surface, if indeed it has a "surface" at all. But at least two moons of Jupiter—Ganymede and Europa—and Saturn's Titan are tempting possibilities.

And beyond Saturn? Humans probably will not travel to those distant reaches very soon. Saturn and Jupiter will be sufficient to keep space scientists and explorers busy for decades, maybe for centuries. Uranus and Neptune are, as far as we know, similar to Jupiter and Saturn. It may be that there will be no need or reason to make manned explorations to those planets.

But Pluto might be another story. The mystery of Pluto's origin and its strange behavior may well draw explorers in the future.

In addition, we humans are curious and stubborn creatures. In the long run, in exploring the solar system in which we live, we will not be put off by the cost, distance, or time such an exploration must take.

One thing is certain. Having already taken our first steps in exploring the vast and wonderful solar system in which we live, we will sooner or later go on to explore every nook and cranny of it. Pluto may well seem like the last of the planets that can be reached, but we may be sure that sometime in the future a ship will start out from earth to make the long journey there. And if to Pluto, why not then to the stars?

GLOSSARY

Asteroids—tiny planets found in many parts of the solar system. They are composed of rocks, metal, or ice and range in size from sand grains to mountains or larger. The *asteroid belt* is a region of space beyond the orbit of Mars that contains many asteroids.

Atmosphere—the envelope of gases surrounding a planet.

Axis—an imaginary line through a planet from its north pole to its south pole.

Constellations—familiar groups of stars in the sky. The Big Dipper and Orion are typical constellations.

Eccentric—elongated or oval-shaped and off-center. The orbits of some solar system satellites (like Neptune's Nereid) and one planet (Pluto) are markedly eccentric.

Ecliptic—the plane or flat surface traced out in space by the earth's orbit around the sun.

Ellipse—a slightly elongated oval. Actually, all planetary orbits are ellipses, not perfect circles.

Flyby encounters—exploratory space flights in which spaceships pass close to planets or their moons without actually orbiting or landing.

Galileo Project—a plan to place a future laboratory in orbit around Jupiter and to drop sensing devices down into Jupiter's atmosphere.

Gas-giant planets—large planets composed mostly of light gaseous materials such as hydrogen, methane, and ammonia. Jupiter, Saturn, Uranus, and Neptune are gas-giant planets in our solar system.

"Grand Tour"—close flyby encounters of a spacecraft with three or four giant planets on a single trip.

Gravitational field—the area of powerful gravitational attraction surrounding a massive object such as a planet.

Gravity—the force that attracts objects to each other.

Great Red Spot—a huge whirlwind storm in the atmosphere of Jupiter, varying in color from pink to brick-red; it was first observed in 1665.

Impact craters—ringlike scars visible on the surface of certain moons in the solar system (including the earth's moon). These "craters" were formed when meteorites (roving chunks of rock and metal) struck the moon in the distant past.

Magnetometer—an instrument for measuring the strength of magnetic fields.

Matter—the solid, liquid, and gaseous material that makes up the stars and planets and interstellar gas and dust.

Metallic hydrogen—under extreme pressures deep in the interiors of the gas-giant planets, hydrogen gas is compressed first into a liquid and then into a solid form in which it is actually a metal.

Orbit—the almost-circular path in space that an object (like the earth) follows around a larger, heavier object (like the sun).

Organic molecules—chemical compounds, sometimes very complex, containing the element carbon. All living organisms are made up mainly of organic molecules.

Plane—a mathematical word for a perfectly flat surface.

Planets—major celestial bodies in the vicinity of a star, held in elliptical paths, or orbits, by the star's gravitational field. The earth and Jupiter, for example, are planets of our own star, the sun.

Retrograde—moving backward in orbit, or in the opposite direction from normal, well-behaved satellites.

Satellite—any object held in orbit around another object. Our moon is a natural satellite of the earth; the earth and Jupiter are natural satellites of the sun. (Russia's *Sputnik* was the earth's first artificial, or human-built, satellite.)

Sensing devices—instrument packages designed, for example, to be dropped through the atmosphere of a planet to measure and transmit information about conditions close to the planet's surface.

Solar system—our own sun, its nine planets, and their moons. Other stars may have similar systems of planets and satellites.

Spectroscope—an instrument that analyzes light given off or reflected by an object. Can detect gases and temperatures in the atmosphere of this object.

Terrestrial planets—small, dense, "earthlike" planets composed mostly of rock and metal. Mercury, Venus, the earth, Mars, and (probably) Pluto are the terrestrial planets of our solar system.

FOR
FURTHER
READING

Anderson, Poul. *The Infinite Voyage.* New York: Macmillan Co., 1969.

Bonestell, Chesley and Willi Ley. *The Conquest of Space.* New York: Viking Press, 1950.

Gallant, Roy A. *National Geographic Picture Atlas of Our Universe.* Washington, D.C.: National Geographic Society, 1980.

Moore, Patrick. *The Atlas of the Universe.* New York: Rand McNally, 1970.

Morrison, David and Jane Samz. *Voyage to Jupiter.* Washington, D.C.: National Aeronautics and Space Administration, Scientific and Technical Branch, 1980 (NASA SP-439).

National Aeronautics and Space Administration. *Voyager 1 Encounters Saturn.* Washington, D.C., 1980. Superintendent of Documents, U.S. Government Printing Office, Washington, D.C. 20402 (Stock #033-000-00817-1).